JN418486

THE WINDOW

THE WINDOW

NANGJA WOO'S COLLECTED POEMS

現代詩文學

창문

주님이 나에게 "창문"이라는 시집을 출판 할 수 있는 기회를 주셔서 감사를 드린다.

"자연"을 가까이 하니 주님과 만물의 밀접한 관계를 보았고; "여행"을 통해서는 인간이 사는 사회에서 다른 점보다는 공통된 점이 더 많이 있음을 배웠고; "삶"을 살아가는 동안 갈등과 온정이 함께 하는 것을 알았고; "사랑" 이라는 상태에서는 천사와 악마가 서로 다투는 것을 경험하였고; "신앙" 생활에 전념하면서 주님께 더 밝은 "창문"을 달라고 기원하였다.

본 시집은 모든 친구와 같이 읽기 위하여 자연, 여행, 삶, 사랑, 신앙, 다섯 편으로 나누었다.

2005. 4. 25

우 낭 자

THE WINDOW

I thank God for providing me with an opportunity of publishing
"The Window," through which

I have befriended *"nature"* so as to discover interdependent relationships between
Him and His creatures; I have gained an insight of observing more similarities
Existing in our international communities when *"traveling"*; I have realized
Our existing social *"realities"* where conflict and peace are inseparable from each other;
I have experienced a psychological domain called *"love"* where an angel and a devil are
Wrestling; and, I have devoted myself to my *"faith"* while asking
Him to help me have a brighter window.

This publication is divided into five sections: *Nature,*
Travel, Realities, Love, and Faith for my beloved friends around the world.

April 25th, 2005

Nangja, Woo

Section 1 Nature

자
연

Section 2 Travel

여행

Section 3 Realities
삶

Section 4 Love
사랑

Section 5 Faith
신앙

Section 1 Nature
자연

일출 SUNRISE

계절 SEASONS

봄비 SPRING DRIZZLE

매화꽃 APRICOT BLOSSOMS

민들레 DANDELION

솜구름 COTTON CLOUDS

억새풀 EULALIA

함박눈 FEATHERY SNOWFLAKES

참새와 나이테 SPARROWS AND TREE RINGS

시간 TIME

일출

어두운 모든 형상들이 밝은 것으로 바뀌면서
아침햇살은 계룡산 골짜기를 비추고 있네.
누가 이러한 신비스러운 광경을 글로 나타낼 수 있을까?

검푸른 물이 진홍색으로 바뀌면서
아침햇살이 다도해를 물들이고 있네.
누가 이러한 색깔을 내는 화가를 흉내낼 수 있을까?

하나의 검은 색이 여러 가지 아름다운 색으로 바뀌면서
아침햇살은 거제도 들녘 모든 풀들을 흠뻑 적시고 있네.
누가 이러한 하나님의 역사에 도전할 수 있을까?

SUNRISE

The sunrise plunges into the valleys of KyeRyong
Altering all dark shapes to brighten ones
Who can describe this mysterious scene of reshaping?

The sunrise penetrates into the water of an archipelago
Transforming aquamarine into crimson
Who can resist this colorful temptation of an artist?

The sunrise saturates all the grasses in the hills of Geoje Island
Replacing the single dark color to a variety of shining hues
Who can challenge the works of the Lord?

계절

봄 기운에 젖어
노란 꾀꼬리가
짝을 부르네.

찌는 여름에
매미가 더위를 시키기 위해
한가롭게 노래하네.

솔솔 부는 가을바람에
귀뚜라미가 달빛에서
추위옴을 노래하네.

차가운 겨울 밤에
쥐가 다락방에서
배고픔을 못 이겨소리내고 있네 .

SEASONS

In the breath of spring
A yellow oriole' s warbling
To call for its mate.

In the summer blaze
A cicada chirps spontaneously
To cool itself off.

In the breeze of fall
A cricket creaks in moonlight
To foretell a cold spell.

In the winter blast
A mouse squeaks in the attic
To signify its hunger.

봄 비

봄비가 내리더니
앞산 뒷산을 파랗게 물 드렸네.

회색구름과 소리 없이 떨어지는 이슬이
모든 것을 노랗게 물 드렸네.

무지개를 타고 오는 천사가 신비한 손으로
모든 것을 그려 놓았네.

SPRING DRIZZLE

A spell of spring drizzle
Has greened all the hills back and front.

Gray clouds and silent dews
Have yellowed all around drop by drop.

An angel riding on the rainbow
Has colored all around with her magic hands.

매 화 꽃

거제도 남쪽
외딴 마을에
매화꽃이 연분홍 향냄새로
내동생에게 미소를 주곤 하였지요.

금년에 핀 매화꽃은
동생 기다림에 너무 지쳐서
잊을수 없는 정 만 남겨놓고
태평양을 혼자 건너 가 버렸데요.

APRICOT BLOSSOMS

In a remote village at the tip
Of the southern part of Geoje Island,
Apricot blossoms used to beam my younger brother
With a fragrance of pale pink.

This year the pale pink petals
Being tired of waiting for his return,
Flew across the Pacific by themselves
With an unforgettable affection left behind.

민들레

새 하얗게
보슬보슬
바람에 흔들거리는
머리털 솜

귀여운 고사리 손으로
살며시 꺾어 보았네
송사리 같은 손으로
살그머니 꺾어 보았네

입으로 후후 불어 보았다
산 넘어 바다 건너
날아가라
멀리 머-얼-리

DANDELION

Swaying softly,
Nodding lightly,
Stood the cotton white
With the fluffy hair.

A cute hand like a baby fern,
Plucked the hairs gently,
Little fingers like minnows
Picked them softly.

Away they were puffed and blown,
Wishing them to be floating afar,
Drifting far, far away
Over the hills and across the sea.

솜구름

덤성덤성
바구니에 구름 솜 가득 담아다가
하늘에 계신
어머니께 드리고 싶다.

물레로 가느다랗게 실을 뽑아
베틀에서 짜가닥 짹가닥
한발 올리고 오른손 왼손 북을 넘어
한뼘 두뼘 짜서

어머님의 솜씨 있는 손으로
예쁜 옷 만들어 엄마 없는 아이에게 입혀주고
외로움에 눈물 짓는 노인 어른들께 따뜻한 이불을 만들어
그분들의 마음이 흐뭇하도록 덮어 주소서.

COTTON CLOUDS

Putting the cotton clouds
Lock by lock into the basket,
Wishing to present them to my mother
Who is resting in heaven.

One foot on the loom
With a shuttle running back and forth,
Slap after slap with busy hands
Fine clothes are woven.

With your adept hands, Mother,
Make pretty clothes for the motherless children,
Make warm quilts for the lonely old folks,
Make their hearts warm all the time.

억새풀

쑤욱 쑥
장대같이 큰 키
깊은 산 계곡에서
두 팔 벌려 넝성이 넘어
파아랗게 나부낀다.

깡충 치마
단발머리 나풀거리며
소 쫓는 계집아이
예리한 푸른 잎에 베인
빠알간 장단지

숨이 차 언덕에 주저 앉으니
까아만 눈동자
눈물이 비오듯 쏟아진다.
내리치는 북풍비 한테
찰싹 뺨 맞고

가까이 있는 소나무가 속삭인다.
"조용히 해, 청개구리가 잠자고 있어"
봄비는 계속 내리고
개구리는 물 논에서
합창을 하고 있다

너
억새풀아
내가 보았듯이
너도 초록빛 드레스 입고
파아란 하늘 다시 보게 될꺼야

EULALIA

Protruded all the way up
To a height of bamboo poles,
A sea of eulalia waved
In a deep valley of a high hill
With open arms stretching over the hill top.

A little girl with a short skirt
Bobbed hair fluttering
Running after cows,
Got scratched in the reddened calves
By the green blades of the eulalia.

Out of breath she plopped on the hill
With tears falling down in rain,
Out of her dark brown eyes.
Rain beats her on her cheeks
With the north wind whirling over.

A pine tree nearby whispered,
"Be quiet. Tree frogs are sleeping."
Spring drizzle never ceased,
Frogs are croaking in chorus
In the watered paddy fields.

You, eulalia!
Hang on there!
In your green dress.
You' ll see a brighter sky
As I have seen.

함박눈

짜박 짜박
짧게, 더 짧게
함박눈 위를 소리내어 걷다가
눈 속에 푹 빠져 걸었네

짜박 짜박 눈 밟는 소리에
웃음이 살며시 다가오네
호호 불어 얼은 손을 녹이고 있을 때
함박눈은 들녘을 하얗게 덮고 있네.

FEATHERY SNOWFLAKES

With short steps
I crunched through the snow
With shorter and shorter steps
I drifted along with the feathery snowflakes.

With a contented smile
I made the sounds of crunching snow.
I warmed my hands with puffs
As the feathery snowflakes were blanketing the field.

참새와 나이테

서쪽 산 넘어
해가 숨어 버린 후
둥지 찾아 모여든 참새 떼들
"얘, 오늘 무슨 재미있는 일들이 많았니?"
"그럼, 많았지" 하고 재잘거린다.

곧 그들은
은행나무 숲 속 사이에서
내일 일을 생각하지 않고 잠들었다
나무의 나이테가 늘어 갈수록
참새들은 나무한테 더 의존하게 되지.

SPARROWS AND TREE RINGS

After the sun set down
Over the mountains in the west,
Sparrows flocked back home to their nests.
"Anything interesting today?"
"Sure enough," chattered the sparrows.

Soon in no time,
They fell fast asleep among the ginkgo leaves
Without thinking of their business tomorrow.
As the trees gain more rings year by year
They' ll nestle up to their mellowing trees.

시간

시간

만물의 법칙

태양 아래 있는

모든 만물을 어김없이 지배하고

창조하면서 기르고, 병을 주면서 멸망시키는

만물을 변화의 법칙에 따라서

당신을 누가 통제하는가?

하나님 만이

시간

TIME

Time

Universal Law

That Never Compromises

Under The Great Sun

Creating, Nurturing, Sickening, and Destroying

By The Transformational Law

Who Controls It?

Only God

Time

성 소피아: 성스러운 지혜의 성당 ST. SOPHIA: THE CHURCH OF HOLY WISDOM

갑바도기아: 초기 기독교 사상의 부활 CAPPADOCIA: A REVIVAL OF THE EARLY CHRISTIAN IDEAS

밧모섬으로 TO THE ISLAND OF PATMOS

에덴의 동산: 나가랜드 NAGALAND: A GARDEN OF EDEN

티벳의 풍장 A SKY BURIAL IN TIBET

몽고가 그렇게 위대한 줄은 미처 몰랐네 I NEVER SAW MONGOLIA SO GREAT

전쟁포로 수용소가 있는 거제도: 크게 건너는 섬 THE POW CAMPS AT GEOJEDO: THE ISLAND OF BIG CROSSING

성 소피아: 성스러운 지혜의 성당

흑해와 연결된 말마라해 옆에
이천칠백여년 전 희랍사람들이 세운
비잔티움이라는 옛 도시가 발달하였고
천년 후 콘스탄틴 대제가 이를 다시 건설하였네.

동로마제국때 외적을 막기 위하여 세운
씨오도시어스와 콘스탄틴 장벽 안에
콘스탄틴 대제 이름을 딴 콘스탄틴노플이라는
옛 도시로 번창하였네.

터키 서 북편 쪽에
골든혼 과 보스포러스 해협을 따라
칠십 여 년 전에 콘스탄틴노플의 공식 이름을
이스탄불로 고친 현대도시로 번영하였네.

지금까지 세 번의 다른 이름을 갖고 있는 이 도시,
이곳에 성 소피아 성당이 감히 가까히 할 수 없는
위풍당당함으로 서 있고, 성당 이름은 해기아 소피아,
즉 "성스러운 지혜의 성당"이라고 말하네.

성당 꼭대기에는 돔 형식인 큰 둥근 지붕
밑은 넓고 올라갈수록 좁아지는데
빛나는 천국같이 위로 굽혀져서
자연광선으로 성당 안을 비추어 주고 있네.

둥근 지붕 밑에 마흔두개의 창문을 달아서
밝은 빛이 성당 안을 밝게 만들어
하나님께 예배와 경배 드리기에
경외감을 일깨워 주기 위함이였네.

성당 안은 다채롭게 장식되어 있고
종교 및 정치 지도자를 찬미하기 위하여
벽, 바닥, 천장의 그림, 벽화, 초상 및
모자이크로 조화롭게 꾸며져 있네.

본당 입구의 넓은 홀에 있는 모자이크는
콘스탄틴 과 저시티니안 황제가 외적을 막기 위하여 세운
콘스탄틴 장벽 안에 있는 도시를 그린 그림에서
아기 예수를 안고 있는 성모 마리아에게 그림을 주고 있네.

저시티니안 황제는 그의 제국에 위대한 종교 건축물을 위하여
황후 지오도라와 같이 많은 돈과 노력을 쏟아
기원 후 537년에 성 소피아 성당을 완성할 수 있었는데
이는 건축 및 공학 면에서 불가사의한 작품이었네.

성당이 명작이라, 비잔틴 궁중 역사학자, 포크피어스는
다음과 같이 말 하였네·

"천장은 순금으로 도금되어서, 아름다움의 극치를 달했고...
성당기둥이 대리석으로 장식 된 아름다움을 누가 예찬할까?...
예배 보러 가는 사람은 이 건축물이 인간의 능력으로 세워진 것이 아니고
하나님의 은혜로 되었음을 알게 되며; 하나님과 대화를 나누고 싶은 마음이 일어나기 때문에,
그 분이 먼 곳에 계시지 않으시고 그분이 선택하신 곳에 꼭 계신다는 느낌을 받게 되시요."

성스러운 지혜의 성당, 소피아 성당이여!
그대는 이천년 동안 모든 풍파를 겪었네,
두 번 화재를 당하였고, 몇 차례 지진 피해를 입었으며
페르시아, 롬바르드, 셀주크 터키와의 전쟁도 지켜 보았네.

천년 동안 기독교 영향 밑에서
그대는 성스러운 지혜로 찬란한 시절을 보냈고,
오토만 터키제국에 의하여 그대 제국이 망한 후에
그대는 이스람사원으로 개종되지 않을 수 없었네.

그대 도시가 세 번이나 이름을 바꾸었듯이
그대는 세 셈족종교의* 다른 점도 지켜 보았네.
마음이 좁은 사람은 다른 점만 보아 싸워 피를 흘리게 하고
큰 사람은 공통된 점을 보고 서로 평화스럽게 살아 간다네.

---

* 세 셈족종교란 "유대교, 기독교, 이슬람교" 를 말함.

ST. SOPHIA: THE CHURCH OF HOLY WISDOM

By the Sea of Marmara that connects to the Black Sea,
There grew an ancient city called Byzantium
Established by the Greeks twenty seven centuries ago,
Rebuilt by Constantine the Great ten centuries later.

Within the Wall of Theodosius and the Wall of
Constantine in Eastern Roman Empire,
There grew an old city called Constantinople
Renamed after Constantine the Great.

Along the Golden Horn and the Bosporous Strait
In the northwestern part of Turkey,
There grows a modern city called Istanbul
Chosen as the official name of Constantinople seven decades ago.

At the same spot in this same city
That has three different names so far
Stands the Church of St. Sophia with an unapproachable dignity,
Informing me of the Hagia Sophia as "The Church of Holy Wisdom."

On the top of the church sits a huge dome
Gradually rising wide below as it reaches higher,
Bending over like the radiant heavens
With natural lighting illuminating the interior of the church.

The natural lighting is created by putting
Forty-two windows around the base of dome,
Which allows an incredible play of light within the church.
Light serves to remind the worshippers of God.

Inside the building all glitter with wondrous designs.
The walls, the floors, and the ceilings of the church
are glowing with slightly faded paintings, murals,
icons, and mosaics to inspire adoration of the
religious and the political figures.

At the entrance to the narthex sets a mosaic
That depicts Constantine and Justinian presenting
The walled city of Constantinople to the Virgin Mary
Holding the infant Christ in her arms.

To create great religious architecture in his empire
Emperor Justinian with his money, devotion, and his
wife, Theodora, was able to complete the Church of St. Sophia in 537
To an architectural and engineering wonder.

The church being a wonder, Porcopius, Byzantine court historian, comments:
"The entire ceiling is covered with pure gold, which adds to its beauty···
Who could tell of the beauty of the columns and marbles with which the Church is adorned?...
Whoever enters there to worship perceives at once that it is not by anyhuman strength or skill,
But by the favor of God that this work has been perfected; his mind rises sublime to commune with
God feeling that He cannot be far off, but must especially love to dwell in the place which He has chosen;." (1)

You, St. Sophia, The Church of Holy Wisdom!
You have got through thick and thin for twenty centuries;
Burnt down twice and damaged by a series of earthquakes,
Witnessed the wars with the Persians, the Lombards, the Seljuk Turks.

You enjoyed your golden days with your Holy Wisdom.
Under the influence of the Christian faith for ten centuries.
Following the collapse of your empire by the Ottoman Turks,
You had to convert yourself into an Islamic mosque.

As your city has had three different names,
You might have witnessed the differences among the three Semitic faiths.
Small men see differences making themselves divisive so as to shed blood;
Great men see similarities making themselves united so as to live in peace.

---

(1) Porcopius (1897). Buildings of Justinian, Palestine Pilgrims' Text Society. pp.6-7, 11.

갑바도기아: 초기 기독교 사상의 부활

갑바도기아, 너의 4천 년 긴 역사에서 많은 변화를 보았지:
기원 전 19세기 아시리아 식민지; 하이티티 왕국에서는
“낮은 땅”으로 불렀고; 페르시아 제국 때는 한 주로써;
알렉산더 대왕이 페르시아 정복 후는 독립 국가로써;
기원 후 17년에는 로마 주로써; 비잔틴 제국 때는 주로써;
셀죽, 오토만 터키제국, 터키 공화국에서는 버림받은 땅.

너 갑바도기아가 이 곳에 있군, 마을도 도시도 아니며
앙카라에서 320㎞ 떨어진 터키 동북쪽 황폐한 곳에 있구나.
너는 1907년 불란서 천주교 신부가 발견하기 전에는
이슬람 통치로 1,000년 동안 역사 속에 묻혀 있었지.
너는 잊을 수 없는 기독교인의 발자취를 가지고
이슬람 땅에서 기독교인을 위하여 명승지 노릇을 하는구나.

기독교는 성 바울이 이 지역을 통하여
앙카라로 갈 때 이곳에 들어왔다고 한다.
마태 및 누가 복음 몇 구절에서 보여주는 초기 기독교 사상:
겸손, 자애, 형제사랑, 마음의 바꿈, 구원.
기독교 사상의 지도자인 성 바울의 공헌을
이곳 갑바도기아 계곡에서 다시 생각나게 하는구나.

“심령이 가난한 자는 복이 있나니 천국이 저희 것임이요...
의를 위하여 핍박을 받는 자는 복이 있나니 천국이 저희 것임이라.” (마태복음 5: 3-10)
“가난한 자는 복이 있나니 하나님의 나라가 너희 것임이요...
인자를 위하여 사람들이 너희를 미워하고 멀리하고 욕하고 너희 이름을
악하다 하여 버릴 때에는 너희에게 복이 있나니.” (누가복음 6: 20-22)

불변하는 기독교 사상에 다신교를 숭배하는
희랍-로마 종교는 사실상 무력화가 되고 말았지.
로마사람들은 기본 욕구인 안전, 평화, 번영을 충족키 위하여
그들의 신들과 적절한 관계를 맺으려고 하였지.
불변하는 사상에 위협을 느낀 그들은 기독교인을 박해하였으나,
그 박해는 오히려 기독교의 조직력을 강화 시켰지.

기독교의 메시지는 불공평한 로마제국 사회와
족쇄를 차고 있는 노예에게 밝은 빛을 주었지.
영생에 대한 약속은 부지, 가난한 자, 노예, 귀족, 남과 여,
유대 및 비유대인 모든 사람에게 평등 의식을 심어 주었고,
서로 돕고 가난한 자, 병든 자, 과부, 고아들을
도움으로써 인간의 기본 욕구를 충족시켰지.

디어더시우스 대제(378-395)때 기독교가 로마 국교로 채택된 후
힘을 얻어 강력한 계급 관료 조직을 바탕으로 성장하여 퍼져 갔네.
그러나 이는 종교 정치 지도자간에 분열과 갈등을 만들게 하였지.
순교시대 정신은 퇴색되어 갔고 교회의 갈등은 몇몇 헌신적인
기독교인으로 하여금 이상적인 곳에서 초기 기독교 사상을 찾게 되었지.

갑바도기아 는 고행 생활을 원하는 사람에게는 이상적인 곳이었고,
아리안 논쟁* 으로 시작된 교회 분열에 실망을 느낀 바실은 니사 교구의
동생 그레고리와 같이 갑바도기아에서 수도생활을 하였고,
그곳에 나지안져스 교구의 그레고리도 동참을 하였지.
바실은 병원을 세우고, 수도생활을 조성하고 예배의식을 개혁하였지.
그가 만든 수도생활에 대한 규범은 동로마제국의 수도생활에 기본이 되었네.

초기 기독교 사상을 좇는 신도는 갑바도기아에 와 가끔
인조 석혈에 살면서 기도, 참회, 단식으로 일생동안 봉사하였네.
지금 이 곳에서 볼 수 있는 것은 지하도시, 바위교회, 석회암으로
조각된 후레스코 벽화, 도자기, 카펫이 있는 예배당이네.
갑바도기아 삼 교부: 바실, 나지안져스 교구 그레고리, 니사 교구 그레고리는
11세기 모자이크 그림으로 러시아 키에브에 있는 성 소피아 성당에 있단다.

앙카라에 있는 숙소로 돌아올 때 예수님의 사상을 전하는데
불변의 진리를 만든 예수님의 제자를 포함한 성 바울을
생각해 보는 기회를 준 갑바도기아에게 감사를 드렸다.
나는 기독교인이라고 하지만, 과연 기독교인으로써 무엇을 하였는가?
성 바실과 그의 친구들 같이 누구보다 먼저 갑바도기아에 가서
나의 죄를 참회하고 나의 인간성을 바꾸어야 겠다.

---

* 아리안 논쟁은 "예수님의 정체가 하나님이냐 또는 인간이냐?" 라는 문제를 다루고 있다.
구원에 관련된 이 문제는 매우 중요하다. 아리안 주의는 알렉산드리아 신부 아리어스 를 추종하는
사람들의 견해로써, "예수님은 인간으로 존재하였기에 정말 하나님이 아니다." 이 주장은
알렉산더 주교 아타나시우스로부터 도전을 받았는데, "예수님은 인간이였지만, 또한 하나님이셨다."
콘스탄틴 황제는 이 논쟁에 심려를 느껴 전체 기독교 전 대표를 소집하여 니케에 종교회의를
기원 후 325년에 열어 아리안 주의를 책망하고 예수님은 신과 "같은 존재"라고 선언하였다.
그러나 니케에 종교회의는 논쟁을 완전히 종식시키지 못하였고, 아라안 주의는 몇몇
동 로마 제국 교회에서 없어지지 않고 있다.

CAPPADOCIA: A REVIVAL OF THE EARLY CHRISTIAN IDEA

Cappadocia with your four thousand years of long history has embraced
A variety of sociopolitical roles: an Assyrian colony in the 1900 BC;
The "Lower Land" of the Hittite Kingdom; Province of Persian Empire;
Independent state after the conquest of Persia by Alexander the Great;
Roman prefecture in 17AD; Province in The Byzantine Empire; and
A neglected land in Seljuk, Ottoman Turks, and in the Republic of Turkey.

Here you are, Cappadocia, neither a town nor a city, but a deserted area
Located at the northeastern part of Turkey, 320 km from Ankara.
During the Islamic reigns of ten centuries, you had been buried in history
Before a French Jesuit priest rediscovered you in 1907.
Now you serve as a landmark for the Christians in an Islamic land
With your unforgettable footprints related to the Christian activities.

Christianity came to this region with St. Paul who passed through on his way to
Ankara. His leading mastermind of the early Christian ideals: humility, charity,
Brotherly love, transformation in the inner person, and salvation
As revealed from several excerpts in the Gospels of Matthew and Luke,
Inspired me to rethink his contribution on those valleys in Cappadocia.

"Blessed are the poor in spirit: for theirs is the kingdom of heaven… Blessed are those who are persecuted because of their righteousness, for theirs is the kingdom of heaven." (Matt 5:3~10)

"Blessed are you who are poor, for yours is the kingdom of God… Blessed are you when men hate you, when they exclude you and insult you and reject your name as evils, because of the Son of Man." (Luke 6:20~22)

For these universal Christian ideals, the Roman religion, a Pantheon of
Greco-Roman gods and goddesses, became virtually defenseless.
The Romans attempted to seek proper relation with Gods so as to satisfy
Their basic needs: guaranteed security, peace, and prosperity.
Threatened by these ideals, Roman leaders began to persecute the Christians,
Which served to solidify Christianity as a centralized institution.

The Christian gospel offered a great deal of bright lights to the suffering and
Unjust Roman world where an increasing number of slaves were shackled.
The promise of eternal life was for the rich, the poor, slaves, aristocrats,
women, Men, Jews and Gentiles: a sense of equality for all peoples.
Christianity satisfied the basic human needs to belong by helping each other
And offering assistance to the poor, sick, widows, and orphans.

After the adoption of Christianity as an official religion of the Roman Empire
Under Theodosius the Great (378-395), it began to grow and spread and stronger
Hierarchical bureaucracy, which created more schisms and conflicts among the Religious and
political leaders. The days of martyrdom faded out, and the days
Of Church conflicts helped some devout Christians to look back on the early
Christian Ideas in an ideal place.

Cappadocia became an ideal place for those who prepared for ascetic life styles.
Disappointed by the schisms of the church caused by the Arian Controversy,*
Basil the Great (329-379) from Caesarea and his brother, Gregory of Nysa
Settled as hermits in Cappadocia where they were joined by Gregory of
Nazianzus. Basil established hospitals, fostered monastery, and reformed the liturgy.
His rule, a code of monastic life, became the basis of Eastern monasticism.

Followers of the early Christians came to Cappadocia to devote their lives to Prayer, penance, and fastening, while living in man-made caves.
Now the visual memories of Cappadocia are underground cities, rock churches, Chapels with their frescoes carved from tufa, potteries, and carpets.
The three Cappadocian Fathers, Basil the Great, Gregory of Nazianzus, Gregory of Nysa are seen in an 11th century mosaic in the church of St. Sophia in Kiev.

On my way to my lodge in Ankara, I thanked Cappadocia for giving me a chance To look back on St. Paul including Jesus' disciples who provided a universal basis For the spread of Jesus' ideas. I claim myself a Christian, but what have I done as a Christian? I should be the first to repent my sin to transform my inner being in Cappadocia as St. Basil, his friends and followers did.

---

* The Arian Controversy refers to the argument of whether Jesus' nature is divine or human. In a world where people were concerned about salvation, this question was critically important. Arianism, a product of the followers of Arius, a priest from Alexandria, postulated that "Jesus had been human and thus not truly God." The postulation was challenged by Athanasius, a bishop of Alexandria, who argued, "Jesus was human, but also truly God." Emperor Constantine, disturbed by the controversy, called the meeting composed of representatives from the entire Christian communities, The Council of Nicae in 325. They condemned Arianism and proclaimed that Jesus was of the same substance as God. However, the Council of Nicae did not solve the controversy, and Arianism has persisted in some parts of the Roman Empire.

밧모섬으로

흰 거품을 남기며
희랍과 터키 서해안 사이에 있는
에게해의 밧모섬으로
통통배는 가고 있네.

에게해는 지중해의 큰 줄기로서
청동기 시대에 크레타 및 주위 섬에서
첫 유럽 문명이 일어나 발달하였고
기원 전 1400년 전에는 희랍으로 들어갔다네.

에게해 동남쪽에 밧모섬이 있는데,
로마제국 때는 귀양처로 쓰였고,
13세기에 베니스 영토로 되었다가,
1522-1912에는 오토만 제국에 점령 당 하였고,
1921년에 이태리에, 1947년에 희랍 영토로 되었다네.

끝없는 수평선을 등진 잔잔한 바다는
푸르다 못해 사파이어 색으로 변하였으며,
옛 도시 밧모 에서 가까운 스카라라고 불리는
조그만 현대식 항구로 가고 있네.

화산 분출로 생긴 섬은 면적이 34스퀘어 킬러미터이고
섬 주민은 약 사천오백명이라네.
대부분의 주민은 관광업이나
또는 감귤류나 올리브를 길러 생계를 유지한다네.

스카라 항구 남쪽에는 밧모 타운 이 있고
11세기에 지었다는 사도 요한 수도원이 있다네.
수도원은 이곳 주요 관광 자원으로
도서실에는 초기 기독교 시대의 귀중한 문헌이 있다네.

스카라 와 밧모 타운 사이에 성 앤 동굴이 있는데
이곳에서 사도 요한이 미래에 대한 계시를 직접
목격하고 제자에게 계시록을 쓰게 하였다는
곳으로 알려지고 있다네.

기원후 95년, 로마제국 황제 도미티안 은
사도 요한 을 밧모 섬으로
18 개월 동안 귀양을 보냈는데
그 동안에 계시록을 쓰셨다는 말도 있네.

사도 요한은 신약 성서의 처음 4 복음서와
세편의 사도 서간의 저자라고 인정받고 있으며,
예루살렘과 에베소의 노년기 생활은 그가 집필하고
소아시아에 교회를 세우는데 도움이 되었다네.

숲이 많지 않은 밧모섬은 나를 웃음으로 반기는데
이에 너무 감격스러워 마음이 아파오네.
그것은 주님의 날을 위하여 계시록을 읽고 보내라고
선택받은 사도 요한의 발자취를 직접 체험할 수 있기 때문이네.

이곳 밧모섬에서
사도 요한 을 다시 만나게 되니
그 분 뒤에서 주님의 음성이 나팔소리같이 크게 들리네:
"너 보는 것을 책에 써서 일곱 교회에 보내라."*

---

* 요한 계시록 1장 9-11절

TO THE ISLAND OF PATMOS

Leaving white wakes behind
The motor boat is heading
For the island of Patmos in the Aegean Sea
Between Greece and the west coast of Turkey.

The sea is an arm of the Mediterranean
Where the first European civilization flourished
On Crete and nearby islands during the Bronze Age,
And spread to Greece before 1400 B.C.

There is Patmos in the southeastern Aegean Sea
Used by the Romans as a place of exile,
Become a possession of Venice in 1207,
Ruled by the Ottoman Empire from 1522 to 1912,
Occupied by Italy in 1912, and awarded to Greece in 1947.

The boat is sliding along the pacific body of water
On the sea woven with sapphire over boundless horizon
To the modern port called Skala
Near the site of the ancient city, Patmos.

The barren island of volcanic origin covers 13 sq. miles
With a population of four and half thousands.
Most inhabitants depend for a living on tourism
Or the growing of citrus fruit and olives.

Just south of the port, Skala, is Patmos Town
With its battlemented Monastery of St. John built in the 11th century.
The main attraction of the island, the Monastery, has a library
Of valuable manuscripts from the early days of Christianity.

The Cave of St. Anne between Skala and Patmos Town
Is considered to be the site where Apostle St. John saw
His prophetic visions of the Apocalypse, and
Dictated the Book of Revelation to his disciple.

Another source says that the Roman Emperor Domitian
Exiled Apostle St. John to this island in 95 A.D.
For eighteen months during which St. John, the son of Zebedee,
Is said to have written the Book of Revelation.

St. John is also credited with the authorship
Of the Fourth Gospel and three Epistles.
His later life in Jerusalem and Ephesus helped
Him write more and found many churches in Asia Minor.

The barren island is greeting me with a sweet smile.
In thrill I grope for the pain in my heart.
It is because I hear, smell, touch, feel, and see the footmarks of St. John
Who was chosen to read and send the Revelation for the Lord' s Day.

Here in this island of Patmos,
I see you again, St. John.
I hear what you heard a loud voice like a trumpet,
"Write on a scroll what you see and send it to the seven churches." *

---

*The Revelation. 1:9-11

에덴의 동산: 나가랜드

오, 사랑하는 친구 나가랜드, 나가랜드 여!
그대가 나를 환영하고 따뜻이 안아 주기 전에는
그대가 어디에 있고 어떻게 생겼는지를 알지 못하였오.
그대의 역사, 명승고적, 관습도 몰랐고
그대의 강, 촌락, 부족 및 자랑도 몰랐지요.

지금은 그대 옆 이웃에 있는 지역들을 알 수 있지요.
서북쪽에 아쌈 주, 동쪽에 미얀마,
북쪽에 아루나찰 프라데쉬 주, 남쪽에 마니퍼 주
깊이 들어간 강 계곡에 있는 울창한 숲과 험한 산들이
그대를 에덴의 동산으로 만들 수 있었소.

인도에 있는 조그만 주* 인 그대는 단시리, 도양,
딕후 강이 그대의 평화스러운 땅을 흐르고 있지요.
나가랜드 산맥은 사라마티 라는 12,000피트에 달하는
봉우리와 함께 장엄한 경치를 뽐내고 있어서,
그대 동산에 또 하나의 아름다움을 갖다 주지요.

방콕에서 캘카타로 비행하고, 그 곳에서 그대의 주요
산업도시인 디마프라 란 도시에 도착했지요.
산마루 꼭대기를 뱀 같이 꾸불꾸불 휘여 감는
험한 도로를 따라 목적지까지는 5시간 이상 걸렸고,
드디어 프체로 라고 불리는 마을이 나의 시야에 들어 왔오.

험한 산맥 위에 있는 이 외딴 마을은 언덕 꼭대기에
두드러지게 높은 터에 세워져 있고
많은 집은 회색 또는 빨간 벽돌로 지어졌고
집으로 통하는 산길 옆을 따라 이름 모를
야생 난초가 자신의 예쁜 색을 뽐내고 있었지요.

문을 열고 반갑게 미소 짓는 얼굴들이 나를 맞으러 뛰어왔고,
광대뼈가 보이고, 반달 눈, 하얀 이, 엷은 흰색 또는
옅은 갈색 피부를 가진 친절한 미모의 얼굴 이였오.
어떤 사람은 다양한 색의 나가 숄을 걸치거나 부족 의상을 입고
소박한 삶을 살면서 진솔한 환영을 보여 주었오.

소박하게 살아 왔기에, 나가랜드 사람들은 사회적 문제가 적어,
개인의 욕심을 채우기 위하여 자기 국민을 교묘히 속이고,
죽이고, 착취하고 사기 치는 정치, 종교, 군부, 기업인도 없었는데,
이러한 옳치 못한 지도자들을 역사에서 많이 보아 왔지요.

소박한 천성을 가지고 살아 왔기에, 나가랜드 사람들은
자기와 다른 점을 넓게 받아들이고 서로 존경할 줄 알지요.
콘약, 아오스, 시마, 안가미스 등 많은 부족은 다른 부족과
훼손 당하지 않은 동산에서 평화스럽게 공존하지요.
오직 인도로부터 독립을 원하는 투쟁은 지금도 계속 되고 있지요.

다양한 언어사용과 신앙도 그대 땅에서는 보장받고 있지요.
영어는 공용어로, 여러 부족 언어사용은 박해를 받지 않으며,
침례교 선교사로부터 들어온 기독교는 이제 다수 주민이
믿는 종교이지만, 전통신앙인 정령신앙* 도 존중 받고 있지요.

인간 존엄성을 위한 평화와 긍지는 그대 땅에서 찾을 수 있으며,
자연이 사람을 차별하지 않듯이, 그대 땅 사람도 사람을
차별 대우를 하지 않지요. 소박하게 자랐기에 훼손 당 하지 않는
에덴의 동산에서 하나님 말씀을 그대는 좇아 살고 있지요:
"네가 얼굴에 땀이 흘려야 식물을 먹고 필경은 흙으로 돌아가리니 그 속에서
네가 취함을 입었음이라; 너는 흙이니 흙으로 돌아 갈 것이니라." (창세기 3:19)

---

* 나가랜드 총 면적은 16,579 sq.㎞(6,400sq.㎞) 인구는 150만
 코히마는 나가랜드 주 수도이며 25,000명의 주민이 살고 있음.
* 정령신앙: "자연은 보이지 않는 힘에 의하여 살아 있다" 라는 신앙

NAGALAND: A GRADEN OF EDEN

Oh, Nagaland, Nagaland, my beloved friend!
Before you welcomed me and hugged me warmly
I didn' t know where you were and how you looked like.
I didn' t know about your history, landmarks, and customs.
I didn' t know your rivers, villages, tribes and pride.

Now I am able to tell who your neighbors are:
Assam Sate on the northwest, Myanmar on the east,
Arunachal Pradesh on the north, and Manipur State on the south.
These mountainous neighbors covered with thickly wooded terrains
And cut by deep river valleys make you form a Garden of Eden.

You, a small state in India, are proud of your clear rivers;
Dhansiri, Doyang, and Dikhu run through your peaceful land.
The Naga Hills boast of their magnificent spectacle with Saramati,
The highest peak standing 12,600 feet high.
The deep rivers and the lofty mountains add extra beauties to your Garden.

I flew from Bangkok to Calcutta, and from there to Dimapur,
One of the leading industrial cities.
We drove on a bumpy road snaking the ridge of the steep hills,
Taking us for more than five hours to reach our destination called Pfutsero.
The village lying ahead far away caught my eyesight.

This isolated village on the rugged mountain ranges is built
In the prominent point along the fold of the hills.
Many houses are structured by narrow and sunken paths leisurely
Approached by confined and sloped footpaths
Along which numerous wild orchids brag of their colors.

Through the gates several beaming faces rushed to greet me.
They were friendly and handsome with high cheek bones,
Almond eyes, sparkling teeth, and pale or brown skin.
Some folks wore colorful Naga shawls or their tribal outfits
Exuding their sincere welcome influenced by their simple lifestyles.

Being nurtured simple, the Nagas have less internal problems.
They have neither crooked political and religious leaders nor
Inhumane military and business chiefs who manipulate, murder,
Or exploit their own people for their personal gains.
We have witnessed those scum everywhere throughout the ages.

Being nurtured simple, the Nagas sincerely respect differences
Among them based on humanitarian love and tender heartedness.
Numerous tribes, Konyaks, Aos, Semas, Angamis, and others
Are peacefully coexisting in your blessed Garden.
Only your advocacy for your independence from India is persisting.

Different languages and faiths are peacefully coexisting in your land.
English as an official language and tribal languages are all respected.
Even your dominant faith, Christianity, introduced in the 19th century
By Baptist missionaries, does not intimidate your traditional faith:
*Animism, which accepts that nature is alive with invisible forces.

As such, peace and pride for human dignity can be found in your Garden.
Nobody discriminates differences among people as nature does.
Your folks enjoy living in an undisturbed Garden abiding by the words of God:
"By the sweat of your brow you will eat your food until you return to the ground, since from it you were taken; for dust you are and to dust you will return." (Genesis 3:19)

---

* Total area of Nagaland is 16,579 sq. km. (6400 sq. miles) with a population of one million and half. Kohima, the capital city, has more than 25,000 inhabitants.

* Animism: The belief that immaterial force animates the universe. Or the belief in the existence of spiritual beings that are separate from bodies.

티벳의 풍장

티벳의 히말라야 산맥에서
양자강으로 흐르는 맑은 강은
반갑지 않은 소리로
나의 방문 목적을 묻는다.

"이 곳에는 무엇 때문에 왔오?"
"물, 산, 대머리 수리를 볼려고요"
"대머리 수리는 왜요?"
"그들은 영의 사자이니까요"

향불 냄새가 코를 찌르고
갖가지 색으로 바람에
나부끼는 부적을 바라 보면서
터벅터벅 산길을 올라간다.

관광객을 위한 전시 코너에서
몇 자루 큰 식칼이 나의 눈낄을 끈다
그 칼은 시신을 토막 내는데 쓴다고 하니
나를 소름 끼치게 하네.

멀리 산 정상에서
장례식이 준비되고 있다.
긴 관악기로 부르면 굶주린 대머리 수리가
빙빙 돌면서 그들만의 만찬을 기다린다.

장례터에 시체가 놓여지고
장례사가 큰 칼로 토막을 내면
곧 굶주린 수리가 게걸스럽게 먹고 나면
단지 갈비뼈와 그 밖의 뼈만 남는다.

남은 뼈는 큰 망치로 부셔서
남은 살과 섞어 놓아
새들이 먹기 쉽게 만들어
죽은 사람의 영혼을 하늘 높이 날아 갈 수 있도록 한다.

자주 빛 승복을 두른 티벳 라마승이
풍장이 행하여지고 있는
산 정상을 물끄러미 잠시 동안 보고 있다.
그 분은 무슨 생각에 젖어 있을까?

"전생, 현세, 내세"에 대한 윤회의 시간 법칙을
중요시 하는 티벳 불교 철학을 생각하고 있을까?
창조하고, 기르고, 병나게 하고, 멸망시키면서
시간은 태양계에 속한 모든 만물을 지배하고 있지.

보통 "현세의 존재" 함이란 윤회법칙에 따라
서로 밀접한 관계가 있음을 말하지.
우리, 죽은 사람, 나는 모두 시간이란 법칙에서 피할 수 없으며
이 법칙은 우리에게 재난을, 연속성과 삶의 방향을 제시하여 주지.

A SKY BURIAL IN TIBET

A clear river leading eventually to the Yangtze River
From the Himalayan Mountains in Tibet
Asks me the purpose of my visit
With an unwelcoming voice.

"What are you here for?"
"To see water, mountains, and vultures."
"Why the vultures?"
"They are the messengers of the soul."

I trudge up the mountain track
With the odor of burning incense
Penetrating into my sense of smell, and
With a sight of many colorful flags fluttering erratically.

At an exhibition corner for tourists
Several huge chopping knives catch my eye.
They are for chopping the corpse into pieces,
Which makes me sick at once.

Over a far reaching mountain summit,
A funeral practice is being arranged.
A long pipe is played as a signal for the vultures
To surround and to wait for their feast.

The corpse is laid out in the burial ground
Where a burial master chops it into pieces with a huge knife.
Soon the ravenous vultures gulp down
Their feast leaving only bare rib cages and bones.

The burial master smashes the bones
With a large hammer, and mixes them with the remaining flesh
To make it easier for the birds to consume,
So that they may soar high with the soul of the deceased.

A Tibetan monk clad in a dark reddish robe
Fixes his eyes for a while on the far reaching summit
Where the sky burial is practiced.
I wonder what he thinks about.

Does he think about the philosophy of Tibetan Buddhism
That values the trans-migratory concept of time:
"Past, present, future?" Yes, time controls everything under the sun
While creating, nurturing, sickening, and destroying.

Each ordinary moment of "being present" is a closely interrelated part
Powerfully conditioned by the law of trans-migration.
The fate of the vulture, the deceased, and I are all destined by Time,
Which provides us with a personal identity, continuity, and direction.

몽고가 그렇게 위대한 줄은 미쳐 몰랐네

베이징 상공을 훨씬 지나니
그림 같은 강, 호수, 초원, 고원, 산들이
번갈아 아름다운 자태를 보여주네.

누런 황토 강은 산들을 유유히 감싸 흐르고
초록색 호수는 산 정상에 앉아있고
"여트" 라는 조그만 둥근 텐트 집이 간간이 흩어져 있네.

둥근 움막집이 그렇게 매력이 있는 줄은 미쳐 몰랐네
"백설 공주와 일곱 난장이" 에서 나오는 집 같이
너무 작고 귀여워서 살고 싶은 유혹을 뿌리치기 힘들었네.

호수가 그렇게 아름다운 줄은 미쳐 몰랐네
수면에 비치는 반짝거리는 햇살이
너무 청순하고 맑아서 나의 마음을 빼앗아 갔네.

푸른 초원과 평원은 그렇게 풍요로운지 미쳐 몰랐네
사람과 가축들에게 먹이가 되면서
오아시스가 띠엄 띠엄 보이면서 기름지고 풍족하게 넓게 펼쳐 있네.

황토색 몽고 고원이 그렇게 장관인 줄은 미쳐 몰랐네
몽고인들에게 오랜 세월동안 삶의 터전인 고원이
서서히 높아지면서 웅장하고 광활하게 펼쳐져 있네.

자연의 아름다움에 푹 빠져 즐기느라,
움츠린 거대한 괴물 같이 멀리서 다가오는
웅대한 누런 고비사막이 다가오는 줄을 몰랐네.

사막이 그렇게 장엄한지 미처 몰랐네
끝없이 펼쳐져 있는 갈색의 모래언덕이
넓고 장엄하고 풍요롭게 보였네.

사막에서 멀지 않는 추운 초원과 평야에서
수 백 년 간 거친 자연 환경을 잘 극복한
용감한 몽고인을 회상하여 보았네.

계절에 따라 초원을 옮겨다니는 유목 생활 때문에
다른 유목민과 싸우게 되고, 거친 자연 조건을 잘 극복하여야 되는
이러한 유목생활이 결국은 호전적 정신을 길러 주었네.

이러한 정신은 싸움터에서 승리하는 기술을 습득하게 되고
이겨서 살아남고, 부, 명예와 권력을 획득할 수 있었다네:
사정거리 무기 사용, 기동성과 작전에서는 아주 탁월하였네.

기병은 보병보다 싸움터에서 유리하며
특수한 말안장과 등자 쇠는 최고의 속력으로 달리는 말 위에서
화살을 빗나가지 않게 쏘는 데 큰 몫을 하였네.

초원의 어느 여트 에서 테무진 은 1162년에,
빨간 돌같이 보이는 피 덩어리를 오른손에 잡고 태어났다고
중국 문헌은 알려주고 있네.

서로 싸우고 있는 여러 부족을 통일 한 후 중국의 북쪽을 정복하고
"전능한 황제" 를 뜻하는 징기스칸 이라는 칭호를 쓰고
1227년 죽을 때까지 정복을 쉬지 않았네.

그의 셋째 아들 오고데이 는 중국의 절반과 고려를 정복하였고
징기스칸 의 손자 쿠빌라이 칸은 중국 전체, 티벳과 페르시아 정복 후
중앙 아시아 초원과 유럽일대를 휩쓸었네.

유명한 장군 바투는 모스코바를 포함한 러시아 제국을 점령하였고
러시아, 폴란드, 헝가리, 그리고 비엔나 근교까지 휩쓸었기에
몽고군의 말발굽이 지나는 곳마다 세계는 공포에 떨었다네.

쿠빌라이 칸 은 역사상 가장 큰 제국을 이룩한 후
법전을 편찬하였고 지폐를 사용했으며
도로, 운하, 우편제도, 고아원, 학교, 병원을 만들었네.

고비사막 허리를 두 팔로 불끈 잡고
비행기는 높은 상공 구름 속을 나르고 있네.
몽고의 모든 영광을 뒤로 남겨둔 채

I NEVER SAW MONGOLIA SO GREAT

After flying high over Beijing,
Rivers, lakes, steppes, plateaus, and mountains
Took turns to present me
With their picturesque views.

Muddy rivers snaked around the mountain ranges,
Several sapphire lakes sat on the tops of the summits,
Beetle-shaped, tiny circular tents called Yurts
Dotted sparsely in-between.

I never saw those ball-shaped tents so enchanting,
Amazingly tiny, cute, and irresistible
As imagined in the setting of
Snow White and the Seven Dwarfs.

I never saw those lakes so gorgeous,
Incredibly fresh, clear, and captivating
With the beaming sunlight
Mirroring from their surfaces.

I never saw those green steppes and plains so sumptuous,
Excessively abundant, rolling, and far-reaching
Dotted with oases, well serving as nurturing sources
For the people and their livestock.

I never saw the burnished Plateau of Mongolia
So spectacular, exceedingly huge, relatively elevated
And extended, well serving as the traditional home
Of the Mongolian people.

Intoxicated so much for awhile with the beauties of nature,
Hardly did I realize that the vast hazel Gobi Desert
Was approaching my eyesight afar
Like a crouching mammoth.

I never saw the sandy land
So beautiful, widespread, grandiose, and lavish
With the endless stretches
Of glittering beige dunes.

I looked back on the undaunted Mongolians
Who have well wrestled with their harsh realities
For many centuries somewhere on the frosty steppes
And plains not far from the desert.

Being nomads, they moved from steppe to steppe
In response to the season struggling successfully with
Their fellow men and harsh natural environment.
The very nature of nomadic life bred into a warlike spirit.

The spirit encouraged them to acquire the excellent skills
Of battle through which they could survive,
And get riches, honors, and power: the masters in the use
Of ranged weapons, rapid movement, and maneuvers.

Mounted warriors having a great advantage over foot soldiers,
Their special saddles and stirrups allowed them
To fire arrows accurately while making good use of
Their top speed and mobility on horseback.

Somewhere in a Yurt, Temujin was born
In 1162 with his right hand holding a lump
Of blood that looked like a red stone,
According to a Chinese source.

He united various warring tribes and conquered
Northern China while taking the title of Genghis Khan
Meaning "The Almighty Emperor." He had a life of conquest,
Lived it, and did not leave it until his death in 1227.

His third son, Ogodei, conquered most of North China and Korea.
His grandson, Kublai Khan, conquered
All of China, Tibet, and Persia,
Swept across the steppes of Central Asia and on into Europe.

The famous general, Batu, occupied Great Russia
Including Moscow, and swept across Russia, Poland, Hungary
To the outskirts of Vienna.
As the Mongols galloped, the world trembled.

After building one of the largest land empires in history,
Kublai Khan set up a code of laws,
Used paper currency, built roads, canals, postal systems,
Orphanages, schools, and hospitals.

The flying machine was trotting along,
Crossing the heartland of the Gobi
With the clouds down and through,
Leaving all the Mongolian glories behind.

전쟁포로수용소가 있는 거제도: 크게 건너는 섬

사랑하는 고향 거제도: "크게 건너는 섬"!
20만 인구를 안고 대한민국 동남쪽 끝에 있는
당신은 저에게 무한한 축복을 주셨읍니다.
당신 품에서 태어나 자랐고, 저에게 신앙과 직업을 주셨지요.
익히 보았던 많은 집, 사무실, 학교 등은 옛 모습이 변하지 않았지요.
그런데 당신 품에 있는 포로수용소가 황폐하고 흉한 모습으로 아직 있어,
사랑하는 우리나라의 어두운 과거사 일면을 생각나게 하지요.

사랑하는 대한민국: "빼어나게 아름다운 나라"!
기원전 2333년 단군이 나라를 세우신 이후로,
당신은 점령, 유린, 합병, 식민지화 되었고, 둘로 갈라졌지요.
한나라 때(기원전 108) 고조선 일부분을 점령하였고,
원나라 때(1231)는 몽고의 군대가 고려를 휩쓸었고,
도요도미 히데요시(1591)는 조선을 침략하여 유린하였으며,
일제는 당신을 합병하고(1910) 2차 대전 말까지 지배 하였지요.

나의 사랑하는 대한민국: "외세에 의하여 분단 된 나라"!
일제의 사슬에서 벗어나기가 무섭게, 당신과 민주에
남아있는 일본 군대를 무장 해제 시킨다는 구실로
당신의 뜻과 상관없이 남과 북으로 강제 분단되었지요.
"공산주의" 라고 하는 사상에 세뇌 된 북한 지도자는
남한을 미국 "제국주의" 에서 해방시킨다는 명목으로
1950년 잘 무장된 군대로 남침을 감행하였지요.

나의 사랑하는 대한민국: "생존을 위하여 싸우는 나라"!
이에 유엔 안전보장 이사회는 즉시 남침을 중단하라고 요구하였고,
트르먼은 미 공군 및 해군 작전을 허가하였고, 맥아더는 인천상륙으로
북한군을 물리쳤으나, 모택동은 영광스러운 승리를 위하여
북한동지를 돕는다고 중공 인민 의용군 파병을 명하여,
3년간 계속된 이 전쟁은 대량의 파괴를 불러와, 인명 사상 6백만,
그리고 전쟁포로 5만 명을 나의 고향 거제도로 이송하였지요.

나의 사랑하는 고향 거제도: "크게 건너는 섬"!
당신은 그 때 세계 이목을 받게 되었지요.
수용소 내에 소규모 싸움이 친공과 반공 포로 간에 터졌지요.
폭동과 소란이 일어났고, 15명의 반공포로는 "인민재판"에 의하여
처형을 당하였고, 수용소 사령관 다드 준장은 인질로 잡혔지요.
이승만 대통령은 반공포로 2만 5천명을 석방하였고,
1만 5천명의 중국 반공 포로는 대만으로 송환되었지요.

나의 사랑하는 대한민국: "휴전상태에 있는 나라"!
산업혁명 후 사회, 정치, 경제 분야 개념을 더 뚜렷하게
하기 위하여, 인간은 "주의" 에 대한 새 용어를 만들었지요.
"무정부주의, 자본주의, 중상주의, 당파주의, 개인주의, 물질주의,
군국주의, 기회주의, 지역주의, 테러주의 등."
이러한 용어는 당신의 통일에 지금까지 큰 걸림돌만 되었지
"휴전"을 종식시키는 데는 아무런 도움이 되지 않지요.

나의 사랑하는 대한민국: "조용한 아침의 나라"!
세계 양차대전 이후, 특히 냉전시대 때, 당신과 평화를 사랑하는
나라들은 이념 충돌로 많은 어려움을 겪었지요.
"주의" 를 말하는 많은 용어들이 개인 또는 특정 그룹의
정치적 경제적 이득을 위하여 종종 남용되었지요.
인간의 이념과 계획은 하나님 지혜 없이는 완전할 수가 없는 법이지요.
"사람의 마음에는 많은 계획이 있어도, 성사시킴은 하나님 뜻에 있노라."*

---

*잠언, 19장 21

THE POW CAMPS AT GEOJE-DO: THE ISLAND OF BIG CROSSING

My beloved hometown, GeoJe-Do: "The Island of Big Crossing"
Located at the southeastern tip of Korea with a population of 200,000.
Thank you for providing me with an insurmountable amount of blessings.
You' re the town where I was born, grew up, obtained my faith and profession.
Many houses, offices, schools known to me for a long time stand unchanged.
But there sit quite a few POW camps deserted and loathsome in my hometown,
Which often prompts me to think of the darker history of my country.

My beloved country, Korea: "The Land of Sparkling Beauty."
Since the age of Tangun, the founder of Korea (2333 B.C.),
You' ve been often occupied, ravaged, annexed, now even split into two.
The Han Dynasty of China occupied part of you in 108 B.C.,
The Mongols during the Yuan Dynasty swept into you in 1231,
Toyotomi Hideyoshi' s soldiers attacked and ravaged you in 1592,
Japan annexed you in 1910 and colonized you until the end of WWII.

My beloved country, Korea: "The land divided by foreign powers"
Following the liberation from the shackles of Imperial Japan,
You were forced to be divided into the two Koreas: North and South,
On the pretext of disarming the Japanese soldiers in you and Manchuria.
North Korean leaders brainwashed their people with a communist ideology
Launched their cross-border invasion with their well-prepared attack
In 1950 on the pretense of liberating the South from US imperialism.

My beloved country, Korea: "The land struggling for survival."
The UN Security Council called for the immediate end of aggression.
Truman authorized US Air and Naval operations, MacArthur repelled
The invasion by landing at Inchon, Mao Zedong ordered the Chinese People' s
Volunteers to support their North Korean comrades in winning a glorious victory.
The war lasted for three years causing massive destruction with 6 million casualties.
As a result, 50,000 POWS were transferred to GeoJe-Do, my hometown.

My beloved hometown, GeoJe-Do: "The Island of Big Crossing."
You became a highlighted spot of world attention.
Within the POW compounds, a mini battle started between the groups of
Pro and anti-communist prisoners. Riots and disturbances instigated, 15 anti-
Communists POWs were executed by the People' s Court while Gen. Dodd, the Camp
Commandant, was captured. President Syngman Rhee Released 25,000 Anti-
Communist POWs, and 15,000 Chinese prisoners Were repatriated to Taiwan.

My beloved country, Korea: "The Land in the Cease Fire."
Since the Industrial Revolution, we have coined many terms based on "__ism"
So as to define ideas related to sociopolitical and economic phenomena such as
"Anarchism, capitalism, commercialism, factionalism, individualism, materialism,
Militarism, opportunism, provincialism, terrorism, and so forth."
These terms have not helped in ending "the cease-fire" so far.
Instead they have served as enormous hurdles for your unification

My beloved country, Korea: "The Land of Morning Calm."

Since WWI & II, and during the period of the cold war, you and other peace-loving

Countries have seriously suffered from ideological conflicts.

Many terms coined with " __ism" have been often misused for personal

Or certain group' s political and economic gains.

Men' s ideas and plans without God' s wisdom is always incomplete as revealed,

"Many are the plans in a man' s heart, but it is the Lord' s purpose that prevails." *

---

*Proverbs 19:21

Section 3 Realities
삶

고난의 삶

강산이
변하고 변하여
육십 년이 다 되어 가네.

가시밭길을
그 동안 맨발로
나 혼자 걸어 왔네.

발이 돌 같이 굳었듯이
내 삶도 단단해져
가시에 찔려도 피 날 곳이 없네.

THORNY LIFE

Nature has witnessed
So many transformations
During the past six decades.

Along the thorny path
I have trampled barefoot
All by myself.

My life has been molded
With my feet hardened as rock.
No thorns can prick them to bleed.

미소

갓난아이의 귀여운 미소를 보게 되면
나는 나의 인간성을 맛보는 것 같네.

어름 같은 차거운 미소를 보게 되면
나는 나의 인간성을 잃어 버리는 것 같네.

햇볕처럼 밝은 미소를 보게 되면
고이 간직한 꿈이 실현되는 것 같네.

꽃같이 향기로운 미소를 보게 되면
꿈 많던 소녀 시절을 보는 것 같네.

에로스 같은 로맨틱한 미소를 보게 되면
사랑하는 연인을 만져 보는 것 같네.

썩은 생선같이 냄새나는 미소를 보게 되면
사기 치는 정치인들을 보는 것 같네.

과부의 슬픈 미소를 보게 되면
나의 마음을 애타게 하네.

할머니의 훈훈한 미소를 보게 되면
하나님 나라에 하나님과 있는 것 같네.

악마와 같은 흉악한 미소를 보게 되면
하나님의 사랑을 잃어버리는 것 같네.

모나리자 같은 미묘한 미소를 보게 되면
하나님의 신비스러운 역사를 보는 것 같네

SMILE

At a smile as sweet as an infant's
I feel like tasting my being humane.

At a smile as cold as ice
I feel like losing my humanity.

At a smile as bright as sunshine
I feel like realizing my cherished dream.

At a smile as fragrant as a flower
I feel like visualizing my unforgettable girlhood.

At a smile as romantic as Eros'
I feel like touching my beloved sweetheart.

At a smile as stinky as rotten fish
I feel like smelling crooked politicians.

At a smile as heartbroken as a widow's
I feel like tantalizing myself.

At a smile as comforting as my grandmother's
I feel like being with Him in His kingdom.

At a smile as malicious as the Satan's
I feel like forgetting His love.

At a smile as subtle as Mona Lisa's
I feel like accepting His mysterious works.

욕망

한 겹 한 겹
욕망은 나를
열 두 겹 감고 있다.

욕망을 채우기 위하여
"물에 빠진 사람 지푸라기라도 잡는다" 하니
실날 같은 생각에 위안이 된다.

위로 받고 싶어
당신한테 소식 듣기를
오랫동안 기다렸는데.

욕망이란 무엇인지?
가진 것이 많으면 많을수록 욕망도 커지는가?
"다 가질려고 하면, 다 잃게 된다" 라고 서양 속담은 말하지.

DESIRE

Layer by layer
Desire keeps binding me
Until in as many as twelve folds.

To satisfy desire
"A drowning man will catch a straw,"
It serves as a solace, though.

With great patience
I' ve long waited to hear from you
So as to be enlivened by your comforting words.

What is desire?
Do our desire increase when our possessions increase?
"Grasp all, lose all" says a Western proverb.

분노

재미나는 일도 없고
따분함에 지치고
일상생활에 지쳐서
화가 나지 않을 수 없네.

화가 쌓여 화산처럼
하늘 높이 치솟고
태평양까지 멀리 퍼지지만
나는 더 이상 참을 수 없네.

분노의 화산은 얼마나 계속 될까?
얼마나 높이 오를까?
얼마나 멀리 퍼질까?
누가 알겠소.

FRUSTRATION

Tired of having unprovoked ideas
Tired of having boredom
Tired of doing the daily routine
I can't help being frustrated.

Frustration masses up like a volcano
Erupting high up to the sky
Sprcading afar to the Pacific Ocean
I can't control it any longer.

How long until the volcano activate?
How long will it erupt?
How far will it spread?
God knows only.

공허

삶은 외로움인지 애착인지?
괴로움인지, 만족인지?
나도 당신도
알 수 없지요.

예배 후 교회가 끝난 후
문이 몇 번 열리고 닫히고
개구쟁이 웃음소리도 들리지 않으면
텅 빈 교회는 적막 속에 쌓여 있네.

EMPTINESS

Is life lonely or affectionate?
Is life distressed or contended?
Neither you nor I
Know the answer.

The congregation breaks up after the service.
The doors repeatedly close and open.
The kids' chattering and laughter arc hcard no more.
Only the hollow church remains in all emptiness.

방향

수평선 한 가운데
저녁놀 햇살이
반짝이는 무늬로
바다를 수 놓고 있다.

나르는 갈매기 노래를 들으며 뱃놀이를 했다.
갑자기 서쪽 하늘이 캄캄해지더니
산더미 같은 파도가 배를 집어 삼키니
갈매기의 노래도 뚝 그쳤다.

비명을 계속 질렀다
"어느 방향으로 헤엄쳐야 됩니까, 동 서 남 북?"
"생명 줄이 비추는 동쪽으로,"
라고 천사는 대답하였다.

WHAT DIRECTION?

The afterglow of the sunset
Garnishes the sea
With a variety of glittering hues
Right in the middle of the horizon.

I enjoyed boating with seagulls with their songs above.
Suddenly the gale and the clouds blacken the sky in the west
While the monstrous waves devour the boat.
The songs of the seagulls immediately silence.

I shrieked and shrieked,
"To what direction should I swim?"
"To the east, the west, the north, or the south?"
"To the east where the plumb-line shines," said an angel.

어머님을 그리워하며

어머님의 장롱을 열면서
저는 울었습니다.
어머님의 성품은 언제나
흐트러지는 때가 없었지요.

당신이 아껴 입으셨던 옷
잘 간수하셨던 뜨게 실
남겨놓은 모든 것 다
동네 사람들에게 나누어 주었지요.

"내가 얼마나 신세를 졌는데요!"
"어머님은 천사이셨지요"
동네 사람들이 그렇게 얘기하며
당신에 대한 추억은 곳곳에 묻어 있지요.

장롱 속 손수건으로
꼭 싸 두었던 십만 천원은
당신이 제일 사랑하셨던 남편, 나의 아버님께,
성경, 찬송, 성경가방 사 드렸지요.

나머지 돈은
당신이 아껴주셨던 정환 학생에게 주어
어머님을 그리워하는 뜻으로
성경책을 사라고 주었지요.

잔돈들은
당신이 사랑하셨던 손주:
에스터, 요셉, 수선, 수진에게
사탕 사 먹게 주었지요.

반지와 목걸이는 어떻게 했냐구요?
어머님의 마지막 뜻을 따라
팔아서 성전 휘장을
만들었지요.

하늘나라에서
"일어나서 빛을 발하라!" 라는 하나님 말씀에
당신은 성전에서 하나님을 뵙고 있지요
그리운 어머님!

IN MEMORY OF MY MOTHER

I had a fit of wailing
When I opened your wardrobe.
Every piece was in perfect order,
Since your nature never allowed disorder.

The clothes you had treasured,
The knitting yarn you had cherished,
Anything else you had left behind,
I distributed all around.

"To your mother, how deeply have I been indebted!"
"Your mother was an angel!"
Townsfolk retell me after you passed away
With good memories about you prevailing everywhere.

The eleven thousand won in the ward
You had covered tight in the handkerchief.
I bought a Bible, a hymn book, and a Bible bag
For your beloved husband, my father.

The remaining Won left in other places
Was given to Junghwan, your beloved student
So that he could buy himself a Bible
In memory of you, mother.

A lot of pennies left around
Were given to your beloved grandchildren:
Esther, Joseph, Soosun, and Soojin
So that they could buy candies.

What about your ring and necklace?
Being well informed of our last wish,
I furnished the church with the curtains
With the money drawn from your jewelry.

God says in His Kingdom of Heaven,
Arise and shed light!
You are having an audience with Him.
My beloved mother!

아버님께

세상일에 불필요한 관심을
전혀 두지 않으시고
오직 흙을 사랑하시며
꾸밈없이 사시는 아버님.

절망 속에서는 더욱 침묵하시고
말없이 저에게 용기와 힘을 주셔서
시를 쓰는데 도움이 되고 있습니다.
관대하심에 감사드립니다, 아버님.

아버님께서는 지금까지 살아 오시면서
정직보다 더 귀중하게 여긴 것이 없었습니다.
"정직하게 살아라" 라는 말씀이
저의 한평생 동안 교훈이 되고 있읍니다.

어떤 때는 공연히 불평하고
화가 나서 말대꾸할 때마다
당신은 침묵으로
움직일 수 없는 큰 바위 역할을 하십니다.

이제 구십 세가 넘으셨는 데도
당신은 저의 큰 지주입니다.
가끔 저는 당신의 깊은 마음을 읽지 못하는데
아버님의 사랑은 제가 가늠하기에는 너무 깊지요.

A REMARK FOR MY FATHER

Fully devoted to plowing a field,
You've led a simple and humble life
Without paying any unnecessary attentions
To our mundane affairs.

When despaired, you are more inexpressive,
From your silence I got encouragement and inspiration
For composing my poems.
Thank you for your silent but generous support, Father.

In your life
Nothing counts so much as honesty.
Your lesson, "Enjoy your honest life"
Has nurtured me all my life.

Sometimes I complain in defiance of you.
Sometimes I grumble in anger at you.
But you have been a huge boulder to me
Immovable in silence.

Now at the age of more than ninety,
You are still my leading strength.
Often I can' t read your mind, Father,
Because your love is too deep for me to fathom.

엄마는 의사

배, 배가 아퍼요 울고 있는
나를 등에 업고
논두렁 길 사이를
왔다 갔다 하였지요.

한 잎 두 잎 쑥 뜯어
절구에 꽁꽁 찌어
수건에 꼭 짜서
초록색 즙을 내어 먹이셨지요.

"자장자장 우리아기,
꼬꼬 닭아 울지 마라,
우리 애기 잠 깰라"
자장가 불러 주시던 우리 엄마

깊은 밤
열이 나서 몹시 신음할 때
하얀 수건 찬물에 담갔다가 꼭 짜서
머리에 올려 주셨지요.

잠들었다 눈을 뜨면
"얘야 괜찮니, 내 새끼?"
내 곁에는, 내 옆에는
날 지키던 엄마가 계셨지요.

MOM DOCTOR

Mom walked to and fro
Carrying me on her back
Who was whimpering with a stomach ache
Along the footpaths between the rice fields.

She plucked mugwort sprouts,
Pounded them in a mortar,
Squeezed them in a towel to get green sap
Which she administered for my stomach ache.

"Hush, hush, hushaby,
Don't cock-a-doodle-doo, you cock,
You might wake up my baby."
She lullabies me to sleep.

Deep at night,
When I was groaning with a fever,
A white towel did she soak in cold water,
To put it on my forehead.

After a short sleep when I opened my eyes,
"Are you OK, my pet?"
Always she was watching me
By my side, by my sickbed.

가족 운동회

뛰고, 기고, 춤추고, 노래하고, 재잘대는
새싹들을 위한
유치원 가족 운동회.

"붕 붕, 따 따 따" 경쾌하게
넓게 멀리 퍼지는 경쾌한 음악소리
벌써 춤추고 싶은 충동을 느끼게 한다.

아빠는 지게에 바지게를 지고
풍선을 쫓아 뛰어 다니고
고사리 손들은 바지게 안에
오색 공을 담는다.

풍선은 터지고, 달리는 경기는 시작되고,
줄다리기, 왁자지껄 웃음소리
떠드는 소리:
"이겨라!" "이겨라!" "우리가 이겼다!"

해가 서산을 넘어
숨바꼭질 하는데,
모든 사람들이 흔적 없이 떠나니
텅 빈 운동장 만 남았네.

AN OUTDOOR ACTIVITY

Just another day for our kindergarten children
Hopping, crawling, dancing, singing, and chattering.
It' s an outdoor activity day for our kids.

"Boom, boom, toot, toot" blared jauntily
The sound of music far and wide,
Which activates us enough to dance to the music.

With A-Frames on the fathers' backs,
Fathers keep running to dodge the balloons,
Kids throw onto the receptacles
On the A-Frames with their tiny hands.

Balloons bursting, race running,
Rope tugging with roars of laughter,
Full of noises: "Let's go! Beat them! We won!"

The sun is playing hide and seek through the clouds
Over the mountain ridges in the west.
All are gone without a trace, leaving the playground deserted.

우정

우정

살아 가는데

없어서는 안되는 소중한 것

사랑하고, 돌보아주고, 믿으며, 서로 나누면

삶이 아주 풍요로와 지네

이것은 누가 주는가?

소중히 간직 하라는

하나님의 선물

우정

FRIENDSHIP

Friendship

Inseparable Relationship

By Ongoing Process

Loving, Caring, Trusting, Sharing

That Enriches Meaning Of Life

Who Is Giving Us This?

It's God's Gift

To Cherish

Friendship

도서실: 가장 가까운 친구

이 세상에서 가장 아끼는 친구가
내 침실 옆방에 있지요.
나는 그를 "가장 가까운 친구" 라고 부르며,
사람들은 도서실이라고 하지요.

낮이나 밤이나, 눈이 오나 비가 오나
나는 필요할 때마다 그를 찾지요.
나는 그를 자주 찾으면 찾을수록
그는 헤아릴 수 없는 지식으로 따뜻하게 맞아 주지요.

가끔 이 문제 저 문제를 하루종일
진지하게 물어보면,
귀찮다거나 불평없이 대해주고
상담료나 보답을 조금도 요구하지 않지요.

내가 어떠한 질문을 하여도
만족한 대답을 줄 수 있는
삼만 권이 넘는 책으로
매일 말없이 조용히 나를 기다리고 있지요.

그의 역할이 하도 많아 열거하기가 힘들지요;
친구로서 나의 길을 올바르게 가는 길을 조언하여 주고,
관광안내원으로서 이 세상 곳곳을 보여주며,

스승으로서 진리를 탐구하라고 격려하여 주고,
현인으로서 하나님의 말씀을 찾고 따르라고 하지요.

네, 그는 정말 우리 문명의 열쇠 이지요;
그를 통하여 국경과 시대를 초월할 수 있고,
그를 통하여 만물의 위대성에 가까이 할 수 있으며,
그를 통하여 모든 어려운 점을 극복할 수 있고,
그를 통하여 나의 편협 된 좁은 마음이 넓게 변할 수 있지요.

자기들의 정치적 목적을 위하여 많은 책을 불 살러 버린
진시황제와 히틀러가 보여 주었듯이
편협되고 속 좁은 사람들은 나의 친구를 두려워 하지요.
문명의 등불인 폭 넓은 사람들은
당신의 가치를 소중히 여기지요.

지식을 얻는 특전을 누리기에는 인생이 너무 짧지요.
건강과 덕행 다음에는 지식 만큼 중요한 것이 없지요.
많은 사람들이 지식 얻기를 원하지만 책을 읽어
노력을 하는 사람이 적으니 슬픈 일이지요
"대저 지혜는 진주보다 나으므로 무릇 원하는 것을 이에 비교할 수 없음이니라."*

---

* 잠언 8:11

LIBRARY: ONE OF MY BEST FRIENDS

Next to my bedroom, there is a good friend
Whom I treasure the most in this world.
I call him, "My best friend,"
Whereas people call him a library.

I can visit him any time I need him,
Day or night, snow or rain.
The more I visit him, the more he welcomes me
With his warm heart and universal knowledge.

Sometimes I stay with him all day long
Asking him this and that question sincerely.
But he asks me neither consultation fee nor anything in return
Without showing any boredom or complaints.

Every day he sits there silently waiting for me
With more than 30,000 wise family members
Including books, journals, references, dictionaries,
All are well prepared to answer any question asked.

His roles are too numerous to be mentioned;
As a friend, he counsels me to live the right way,
As a tour guide, he shows me every corner of the world,
As a mentor, he encourages me to inquire truth,
As a sage, he inspires me to seek and follow His words.

Yes, indeed, he is a set of keys for our civilization;
Through him I can cross the centuries as it does national boundaries,
Through him I can neighbor with greatness,
Through him, I can get through all weathers,
Through him my small-scale mind can be transformed into a large-scale one.

Small-scale individuals often fear my best friend
As evidenced by Emperor Shih Huang-ti and Hitler
Who burnt books in fear of their political foes.
Large-scale individuals, the lamp bearers, cherish
My friend for the development of our civilization.

No life is long enough to exhaust the privileges of getting knowledge.
Nothing after health and virtue is more estimable than wisdom.
It is sad to know that many wish to acquire
Knowledge and wisdom without pains.

"For wisdom is better than rubies, and all things desirable are not to be compared to her." *

---

* Proverb 8: 11

어린이는 무엇을 배우며 자랄까요?

오만하게 자라게 되면
경멸함을 배우게 되지요.

겸손하게 자라게 되면
분별함을 배우게 되지요.

기만 속에서 자라게 되면
배반함을 배우게 되지요.

정직 속에서 자라게 되면
신뢰를 배우게 되지요.

적개심 속에서 자라게 되면
폭력을 배우게 되지요.

편견을 보고 자라게 되면
좁은 마음가짐을 배우게 되지요.

사랑을 받고 자라게 되면
너그러운 마음가짐을 배우게 되지요.

위대한 사람의 말씀을 듣고 자라면
지혜를 배우게 되지요.

물질만능 속에서 자라게 되면
이기심을 배우게 되지요.

하나님의 말씀 속에서 자라면
삶의 참 뜻을 찾게 되지요.

A CHILD GROWS UP WITH WHAT?

A child who grows up with arrogance
Will learn to be contemptuous.

A child who grows up with modesty
Will learn to be reasonable.

A child who grows up with deception
Will learn to be treacherous.

A child who grows up with honesty
Will learn to be trustworthy.

A child who grows up with hostility
Will learn to be violent.

A child who grows up with the words of great men
Will learn to be wise.

A child who grows up with prejudice
Will learn to be narrow-minded.

A child who grows up with love
Will learn to be generous.

A child who grows up with materialism
Will learn to be egocentric.

A child who grows up with the words of God
Will learn to find the meaning of life.

내일은 다르지

몇 주 전 돌담을 쌓았다.
한 개 두 개
모두 천팔백이십오 돌덩어리로.

돌담은 어젯밤 강풍에 무너졌다.
무너진 참상을 보니
실망과 분노에 휩싸였다.

"오늘밤 폭풍이 몰아 친다" 라고 기상예보는 말하는구나.
"그래, 올 테면 와 보라지.
내손으로 다시 쌓을 테야."

강풍은 어젯밤 나를 때려 눕혔으나
이번에는 안되지, 안되지.
내일은 다르지, 다르지.

TOMORROW IS A NEW DAY

A few weeks ago I built a stone wall
Pilling up rocks one upon another
Working with 1,825 pieces.

Last night the wall was collapsed by a gale,
Which made me so furious and disappointed
At the sight of destruction.

"A gale will attack us tonight with a thunderstorm," says a meteologist.
"Gosh! Let him come if he really wants.
I' ll fight back with my own hands, piling up the pieces again and again."

He knocked me down last night.
But not this time, not this time.
Tomorrow is a new day!

Section 4 Love
사랑

사랑이란?	LOVE IS WHAT?
사랑의 기쁨	AN ECSTASY OF LOVE
사랑의 짐	THE BURDEN OF LOVE
네, 물론이지요!	YES, CERTAINLY!
님을 보내지 않았소	I DIDN'T SEND YOU AWAY, DEAR!

사랑이란?

당신을 알게 되었습니다.
당신을 좋아하게 되었습니다.
당신을 사랑하게 되었습니다.
당신을 미워하게 되었습니다.

그러나 “사랑”과 “미움”의
다른 점을 구별할 줄은
아직 알지 못합니다.
알게 되면 말하여 드릴께요.

LOVE IS WHAT?

I've learned to know you.
I've learned to like you.
I've learned to love you.
I've learned to hate you.

But, I haven't learned enough
To tell you the differences
Between "love" and "hatred."
I'll tell you when I am ready.

사랑의 기쁨

연인의 밝은 미소에
나의 눈빛은 빛나고 있네.

사랑을 속삭이는 말이
내 귀속을 흐뭇하게 울리네.

향내 나는 소나무 냄새에
내 코는 벌룩 거려지네.

귀여운 어린아이를 안으면
내 손가락 끝이 짜릿하네.

결혼 예식을 보게 되면
내 심장이 뛰네.

이러한 감동에 흠뻑 젖어 있을 때는
나의 숨소리가 멈추려 하네.

AN ECSTASY OF LOVE

My eyes sparkle
At the sight of my sweetheart' s smile.

My ears tingle
At the sound of romantic words.

My nostrils quiver
At the scent of fresh pine trees.

My finger tips thrill
At the touch of a cute baby.

My heart throbs
At the scene of a wedding ceremony.

My breath is about to be taken away
At the mood of being intoxicated.

사랑의 짐

저의 무거운 사랑의 짐을
당신께 내려놓습니다.
당신이 맡으시라고요.

저의 아픈 사랑을
당신께 맡깁니다.
당신은 사랑이 무엇인지 아시니 까요.

THE BURDEN OF LOVE

Let me unload my burden
That is too heavy for me.
Instead, place it in your charge.

Let me entrust my tantalizing love
To your tender care, dear.
Because you know what it is.

네, 물론이지요!

당신 앞에는
오직 당신 앞에서는
이 한 마디 만 분명히 드리고 싶습니다.
"당신을 사랑합니다."

당신께서
무엇을 하라고 말씀하시면
당신께 드릴 말은:
"네, 물론이지요."

YES, CERTAINLY!

To you
Only to you,
This word I'd like to say clearly:
"I love you, dear."

Should you bid me to do anything,
My answer shall be:
"Yes!"
"Yes, certainly."

님을 보내지 않았소

우리 태평양 바다를 건널 때
넓고 넓은 대지에서
꿈을 펼치자고
약속하였지요.

님은 밀어주고
나는 이끌어 주고
지쳐서 쓰러질 때까지
우리는 열심히 뛰였지요.

사랑은 뜨거운 여름 밭에
무르익은 참외같이
더욱 더 무르익어 가
우리는 우뚝 설 수 있었지요.

어느 으스스한 가을 날
나뭇잎이 우수수 떨어 질 때
님은 작별 인사 없이 떠나 버리고
나의 마음을 천 갈래 찢어 놓았지요.

그러나 님의 맥박은 나의 가슴속에 뛰고 있고
님의 숨결을 아직 느끼고 있으며
님의 말은 내 마음속에 살아있고
님의 정열은 내 핏속 깊이 흐르고 있지요.

님을 하루도 그리워하지 않는 날은 없었고,
님을 한시도 원망하지 않을 때가 없으며,
님을 잠시도 사랑하시 않을 때가 없었소.
님을 떠나 보내지 않았소!

I DIDN'T SEND YOU AWAY, DEAR!

When we sailed across the Pacific
So vast, so boundless,
We agreed to achieve our dreams
In the wide and virgin world.

You pushing me behind
Me pulling you ahead,
We dashed everywhere
Until the day we're worn out.

Our love grew to be mellow
As the yellow melons in the summer field.
An aspiration of love warm and deep
We stood aloof.

On a chilly autumn day
When the leaves started falling down,
You left me without saying good-bye
Breaking my heart into pieces.

But your pulse still beats in my heart,
Your breath still pervades me,
Your romantic words are still alive within me,
Your passion still runs deep in my veins.

Not a single day has passed without thinking of you.
Not a single hour has passed without grudging you.
Not a single minute has passed without loving you.
I didn't send you away, dear!

Section 5 Faith
신앙

기도

주님, 동방 땅 끝
해 뜨는 나라에
살게 해 주셔서
감사드립니다.

주님, 폐허가 된
소 아시아 옛 일곱 교회들까지
선교의 눈을 뜨게 해 주심에
감사드립니다.

PRAYER

Thank Thee, my Lord
For providing me with a place to live
In the land where the sun rises
At the tip of the Far East.

Thank Thee, my Lord
For providing me with a mission to spread Thy words
Even to the land where the seven ancient churches in Asia Minor perished.
I can never thank Thee enough.

은총에 대한 감사

주님, 태고 때부터 지금까지
주님의 뜻인 변화의 법칙에 따라
강산은 변하고 있습니다.

주님이 주신 큰 빛이
얼음장을 사르르 녹이고 있듯이
저의 마음도 변화를 갖다 줍니다.

주님 앞에 무릎을 꿇고 기도합니다
얼음장을 녹여 따뜻한 사랑으로 바꾸어 주신
주님의 큰 빛에 크나 큰 감사를 드립니다.

THANKS FOR YOUR GRACE

Lord, from the time immemorial,
Nature has been transformed
By Your design, the law of transformation.

As the great light furnished by You
Is melting the ice, frozen hard,
So is my heart getting gradually warmed by Your grace.

Lord, I pray unto You on my knees,
I am giving You all my thanks for Your light
That is transforming ice into warm love.

주여! 당신의 것입니다.

이 넓고 불안한 세상에
저는 오직 주님과 같이 있습니다.
잠을 깨면, 주님하고 불러 보면서
외로움을 달래고 있습니다.

주님께 가끔 트집을 부렸습니다.
제 마음이 괴로워 터지도록 아플 때
생트집을 부리고 울면서
주님의 마음을 아프게 하였습니다.

산다는 것은 너무 어려워
때로는 죽고 싶은 충동도 느꼈습니다.
밤이 새도록 울고
당신 앞에 위로 받으러 매달렸습니다.

때로는 주님과의 약속을 어기고
옆길로 걷고 있었습니다.
생활에 너무 지치고, 주님의 말씀을 따르기가 힘들어
쉬운 길을 택하였읍니다.

저는 주님의 것이라는 것을 알고
이제 주님의 품으로 돌아 왔습니다.
어떠한 어려움이 따르더라도
각오하고 따라가겠습니다.

주님이 저를 붙들어 주시면,
못 할 일도 없으며,
무서워 할 것도 없으며,
필요한 것이 아무 것도 없습니다.
주여, 인정하여 받아 주십시오.

I AM FOR YOU, MY LORD!

In this wide and unpredictable world
I abide by You only.
When I am awake, I call for You to be with me
So that I may not be lonely at all.

I often blamed You, my Lord.
When in heartrending agony,
I burst out wailing in obstinacy
Hurting Your heart.

Life has been very thorny for me.
Sometimes I wish I were dead,
Sobbing all night long
Turning to You for relief.

Sometimes I walked along the wrong way
Against my promise to You.
Being too exhausted, I preferred an easier way.
Because Your words seemed to be impossible to follow.

Now I'm back home under Your grace,
Realizing that I am for You, my Lord.
I am determined to follow You
No matter how difficult it may be.

When Your arms uphold me,
There is nothing I can't do,
There is nothing I fear,
There is nothing I evaid,
Please accept me, my Lord!

새벽 기도 가는 오솔길

아직 어두컴컴한 이른 새벽녘에
달빛과 어둠이
이 세상을 차지하려고
서로 씨름하고 있을 때
새벽 기도 가곤 하지요.

얼마 후면 어둠과 달빛이 사라지게 되는데:
"어둠 아저씨, 나의 빛으로 모든 것을 아름답게 비췄지요,"
달이 자랑스럽게 말하니,
"그래요? 나도 어둠으로 그렇게 했는데요, 달 아가씨,"
라고 어둠이 대답한다.

은은한 달빛 아래
산꼭대기는 멀리 흐리게 보이고
키 큰 병사 같은 소나무 숲은 나를 포위하고,
조용한 마을의 집 지붕은
달빛에 흠뻑 젖어 있네요.

주님, 이렇게 무한하고
아름다운 선물을 주셔서 감사를 드립니다:
달, 산꼭대기, 셀 수 없이 많은 창조물들을
주님, 이제 더 이상 파괴가 없도록 하여 주시고
아름다운 모든 창조물들의 보존을 위하여 기도 드립니다.

ON MY WAY TO PRAYER

On my way to prayer,
Early, early in the morning,
There is a wrestling match
Between the darkness and the moonlight
For the domination of this world.

Before long, both of them will retire from their roles
On the stage naturally prepared;
"Mr. Darkness, I disclosed all the creatures with my light," brags the moon.
"Oh, yeah? I did the same thing with my darkness",
Miss Moon," responds Mr. Darkness.

Under the retiring moonlight
The mountain summits are indistinctly visible from afar,
The pine forest surrounds me like an army of tall soldiers standing,
The roofs of the village houses are soaking
In the silent rain of moonlight.

Thank Thee, my Lord
For providing me with such beautiful and boundless gifts:
The moon, the mountain summits, and unlimited numbers of creatures.
Please leave them as they are; they are unspoiled.
No more horrible destruction on this world, my Lord.

첫 번째 손님

꼬마가, "두 분 손님이 오셨어요?" 라고 알려 주었다.
일터와 집이 없는 젊은 두 남자
"주실 것이 없으면, 차비라도 도와 주십시요."

그들은 이 달에 주님께서 보내주신
첫 번째 손님
"고맙습니다."
"많이 도와 주지 못해서 미안합니다."

전지 전능 하신 주님,
천지 만물이 당신의 것이지요.
제가 가진 것 이상을 가난한 사람들에게
골고루 나누어 줄 수 있는 힘을 주십시요.

THE FIRST TWO VISITORS

"Two visitors are here," said a little kid.
Two jobless and homeless young fellows begged for help;
"If nothing to spare, bus fare will do."

They are the first two visitors God sent me this month.
"Thank you for your generous help."
"Not at all. I am awfully sorry
Because my alms for you are too meager."

Lord, You are the Almighty.
Everything in the universe is Yours.
Bestow me with strength to help the poor,
Strong enough to give more than I can afford.

기다림

주님 오심을
문 활짝 열어 놓고,
등불 들고 기다릴께요.

주님 오심을
손 꼽아,
기다릴께요.

WAITING

I'm waiting for Your visit, Lord
With my doors wide open,
Bearing a bright lantern.

I'm waiting for Your visit, Lord
Counting on my fingers,
Eagerly awaiting Your calling.

작은 기도원

작은 기도원 가까이에 있는
청순한 흰 마가렛 꽃 향기에 취하고 있다.

기도원에 멀지 않는 물 논에는
개구리들이 합창 연습이 한창이다.

무릎 끓어 기도합니다.
"주님, 넓은 일터로 언제 떠날 수 있을까요?"
몹시 기다려 집니다.

A SMALL ORATORY

I enjoy being intoxicated by the aroma
Of a pure white marguerite near a small oratory.

In the watered paddy fields not far from the oratory,
Frogs are busy in their chorus.

I pray on my knees:
"Lord, when can I leave this oratory for a more challenging place?"
I'm impatient, Lord.

국적 취득은 어떻게?

중국 국적을 얻을 수 있나요?
예, 이민 수속을 따름으로써.

인도 국적을 얻을 수 있나요?
예, 이민 수속을 따름으로써.

이스라엘 국적을 얻을 수 있나요?
예, 이민 수속을 따름으로써.

태국 국적을 얻을 수 있나요?
예, 이민 수속을 따름으로써.

사우디 아라비아 국적을 얻을 수 있나요?
예, 이민 수속을 따름으로써.

하나님 왕국의 국적을 얻을 수 있나요?
예, 하나님 말씀을 따름으로써.

HOW CAN I GET MY NATIONALITY?

Can I get a Chinese nationality?
Yes, by following her naturalization procedures.

Can I get an Indian nationality?
Yes, by following her naturalization procedures.

Can I get an Israeli nationality?
Yes, by following her naturalization procedures.

Can I get a Thai nationality?
Yes, by following her naturalization procedures.

Can I get a Saudi Arabian nationality?
Yes, by following her naturalization procedures.

Can I get a nationality of His Kingdom?
Yes, by following His Words.

나의 창문

하늘에 계시는 하나님!
나의 창문을 닫고
하나님 말씀을 읽었을 때
나와 신앙이 다른 사람들은
사탄의 자녀라고 간주하였습니다.

하늘에 계시는 하나님!
나의 창문을 절반 쯤 열고
하나님 말씀을 다시 읽었을 때
나와 신앙이 다른 사람도
나의 형제, 자매라고 믿기 시작하였습니다.

하늘에 계시는 하나님!
나의 창문을 활짝 열고
나와 신앙이 다른 사람도
결국 하나님의 자녀라고 깨닫기 시작하였습니다.

MY WINDOW

Oh, Lord, high up in heaven!
When I read Your Words
With my window closed,
I began to presume
That those people with different faiths
Are the children of Satan.

Oh, Lord, high up in heaven!
When I reread Your Words
With my window half-open,
I began to believe
That those people with different faiths
Are my sisters and brothers.

Oh, Lord, high up in heaven!
When I understood Your Words
With my window wide open,
I began to realize
That those people with different faiths
Are all Your children ultimately.

About The Author

1971-Present: Minister at GeoSeong Christian Church &
Director at Big Star Kindergarten
GeoJe City, The Republic of Korea

2004: Debuted as a poet from The Contemporary Poetry Quarterly Periodical

1997: Ed. D. in Education (Honorary)
Graduate School of Education
GMP Christian University, Nigeria

1990: Master of Arts in Christian Ministry
Trinity Theological Seminary
Newburgh, Indiana, USA

1986: Ordained

1985: Bachelor of Arts in Music
Bible College Seminary
Los Angeles, CA. USA

THE WINDOW

재판. 2011년 7월 7일
지은이: 우낭자
발행인: 양태철
편집인:김평엽
펴낸곳: 현대시문학사

주소: 서울특별시 은평구 역촌동 37-2 2층
전화: 02-512-0246
팩스주문: 02-512-0182
E-mail: hihd@paran.com
등록: 1999.6.11 제 13-619호

ISBN 89-90520-21-5+03810